Campbell's

EASY

HOLIDAY
COOKING

FOR FAMILY & FRIENDS

For sending us glassware, flatware, dinnerware, oven-to-tableware and serving accessories used in recipe photographs, a special thanks to: *Corning Consumer Products Company,* Corning, NY on pages 48-49; *Dansk International Designs Ltd.,* Mount Kisco, NY on pages 43, 73 and 85; *The Denby Pottery Company,* New York, NY on pages 55, 64-65 and 71; *Fitz and Floyd,* Dallas, TX on pages 13 and 29; *Lenox China and Crystal,* Lawrenceville, NJ on pages 57 and 69; *Mikasa,* Secaucus, NJ on pages 25 and 41; *Nikko Ceramics, Inc.,* Wayne, NJ on pages 37 and 59; *Noritake,* New York, NY on pages 6-7; *Oneida Silversmiths,* Oneida, NY on pages 30-31, 45, 47, 48-49, 69, 75, 79 and 87; *The Pfaltzgraff Co.,* York, PA on pages 19, 37, 89 and 91; *Spode,* Moorestown, NJ on page 63; *Swid Powell,* New York, NY on pages 77, 79, 87 and 91; *Taitù,* Dallas, TX on pages 21, 30-31, 47, 80-81; *Tupperware®,* Orlando, FL on page 27; *Villeroy & Boch,* Princeton, NJ on pages 11, 35, 45 and 53.

This edition is a revised and enlarged version of the soft-cover *Campbell's Easy Holiday Cooking.*

Campbell's Easy Holiday Cooking was produced by the Publishing Division of Campbell Soup Company, Campbell Place, Camden, NJ 08103-1799.

Senior Managing Editor: Pat Teberg

Assistant Editors: Ginny Gance, Peg Romano

Marketing Managers: Mike Senackerib, Brent Walker

Consumer Food Center: Peggy Apice, Jane Freiman

Photography: Peter Walters Photography/Chicago

Photographers: Peter Walters, Peter Ross

Photo Stylist/Production: Betty Karslake

Food Stylists: Lois Hlavac, Lee Mooney, Gail O'Donnell

Designed and published by Meredith Custom Publishing, 1912 Grand Avenue, Des Moines, IA 50309-3379. Printed in Hong Kong.

Pictured on the front cover: Holiday Spice Ring (*page 26*) and Shortcut Chicken Cordon Bleu (*page 40*).

Preparation and Cooking Times: Every recipe was developed and tested in the Campbell's Consumer Food Center by professional home economists. Use "Chill Time," "Cook Time" and/or "Prep Time" given with each recipe as guides. The preparation times are based on the approximate amount of time required to assemble the recipes *before* baking or cooking. These times include preparation steps, such as chopping; mixing; cooking rice, pasta, vegetables; etc. The fact that some preparation steps can be done simultaneously or during cooking is taken into account. The cook times are based on the minimum amount of time required to cook, bake or broil the food in the recipes.

Campbell's *EASY* HOLIDAY COOKING

HOLIDAY MEMORIES ARE
More Than Just Snapshots of the Kitchen

By the fireside or beneath the fireworks. Spreading the cheer of the season or cheering the final touchdown of the season. Indulging in familiar customs or wearing funny costumes. Making a wish over the candles or breaking the wishbone. Holiday scenes and special occasions like these throughout the year make fond memories for family and friends.

If you're the hardworking host or hostess, though, the memories of entertaining a hungry holiday crowd often amount to blurred snapshots of cooking, serving and cleaning up—and a few scattered conversations between trips to the kitchen. Campbell's deliciously easy holiday menus and creative, timesaving party planning ideas combine to escort a very important guest to the party: *you.*

Whatever the season, whatever your reason for celebrating, all of us at Campbell extend you a hearty invitation to relax and enjoy the festivities. Now file away those weary old snapshots of holidays past, smile for the group portrait, and say *Thanks for the memories!*

EASY PARTY-PLANNING TIPS
Set the Table for Memorable Occasions in Your Home

Company Time... Fine china or paper plates? In the parlor or on the patio? Buffet or sit-down? Afternoon or evening? Engraved invitations or a casual phone call? Decisions, decisions. But when it comes to entertaining, you want to dazzle your guests with the frills and flourishes that fit your party pocketbook. That's why with enough preparation time and basic organizing — and a touch of your own imagination — you can have a budget-friendly celebration that keeps you out of the kitchen and in the company of your guests where you belong.

Checking Account... Keep track of party planning by making separate lists for invitations/guest RSVPs, food shopping, serving dishes, tableware needed and decorations. Check off items from each list as soon as they are completed. Take along all the lists when shopping for the party so that you can coordinate and consolidate the various elements where appropriate.

Theme Team... Depending on the occasion, brainstorm theme ideas with a few friends. Holidays become their own themes, but anniversaries, birthdays, graduations, retirements, wedding or baby showers — even get-togethers of friends or family — lend themselves well to individual or group personalization. Be creative with centerpieces, table coverings, entertainment, balloons, candles, banners or memorabilia that might be special to the guest of honor. Choose foods and garnishes that complement each other; offer variety in color, flavor and texture; and are suitable to the serving style.

Steer Away from a Collision Course... Sit-down serving is the most comfortable for guests and works well with smaller groups. But buffet service offers nearly unlimited flexibility for guests *and* hosts. Arrange the buffet table in the following order: plates, main course, side dishes, flatware and napkins. If possible, set up a separate table for beverages away from the food station.

The Count and the Amount... Whether you telephone or send written invitations, do so three to four weeks in advance. Include a deadline for guests to RSVP at least three days before the party date so that you have enough time to plan accordingly for quantity of food, seating space, etc.

That's Entertainment... There are dozens of delightful menu suggestions, creative theme ideas and of course, delicious, timesaving Campbell's recipes included in this book to help you create the mood and the food for any entertaining occasion. *Happy Holidays!*

QUANTITY PARTY PLANNING GUIDE

Beverages . . . . .Servings

COFFEE (6 oz./serving)
   1½ cups ground coffee .12
PUNCH, CIDER OR EGGNOG
   (8 oz./serving)3 quarts 12
SOFT DRINKS
   (6 oz./serving) 2 liter bottle 10
ICE CUBES
   (4 oz./serving) 5 pound bag 20

Appetizers

DIPS (2 tablespoons/serving)
   1 cup dip 8
CHIPS (1 oz./serving)
   1½ pounds 24
CHEESE SLICES (1 oz./serving)
   1½ pounds 24
CRACKERS
   1 pound 24
VEGETABLES (Allow 4 to 6 "dippers"/serving)
   2 lb. broccoli or cauliflower . . . . .32 flowerets
   1 lb. carrots . . . . .65 sticks
   1 pt. cherry tomatoes . . . . .25 tomatoes
   1½ lb. cucumber .50 slices
   1 lb. zucchini (2 medium) . . . . .50 slices

Shortcut Snacks & Sweets

Mouthwatering appetizers are just the beginning of every special occasion! Make a great first impression with zesty *Mexicali Dip*, crowd-pleasing *Party Meatballs* or *Souper Mushroom Pizza* at your next holiday Open House or Super Bowl bash.

Little ghouls and goblins will find *Crunchy Chicken Nibbles* and *Jack-O'-Lantern Cupcakes* frightfully good snacking, too! (*Pictured on page 13.*)

Pictured clockwise from top left: Souper Mushroom Pizza (page 16), Orange Mist, Mexicali Dip and Party Meatballs (pages 8-9).

HOLIDAY OPEN HOUSE

Party Meatballs

•

Mexicali Dip
(p. 9)

•

Souper
Mushroom
Pizza (p.16)

•

Orange Mist
(p. 9)

PARTY MEATBALLS

  1 **can (11⅛ ounces) CAMPBELL'S condensed Italian Tomato Soup**
  1 **pound ground beef**
  ¼ **cup dry bread crumbs**
  1 **egg, beaten**
  1 **tablespoon Worcestershire sauce**
  ½ **cup water**
  2 **tablespoons vinegar**
  2 **teaspoons packed brown sugar**

• In large bowl, mix *thoroughly ¼ cup* soup, beef, bread crumbs, egg and Worcestershire sauce. Shape firmly into 48 (½-inch) meatballs. Arrange in 15- by 10-inch jelly-roll pan.

• Bake at 350°F. for 15 minutes or until meatballs are no longer pink.

• In 3-quart saucepan, combine remaining soup, water, vinegar and sugar. Over medium heat, heat to boiling. Reduce heat to low. Cover; cook 5 minutes, stirring occasionally. Add meatballs; heat through, stirring occasionally. If desired, garnish with *fresh oregano.*

MAKES **48** APPETIZERS
PREP TIME: **20** MINUTES   COOK TIME: **25** MINUTES

Party Frankfurters: Substitute *1 pound frankfurters,* cut into 1-inch pieces, for meatballs. Add frankfurters to soup mixture before heating.

Mexicali Dip

1 can (11½ ounces) CAMPBELL'S condensed
    Bean with Bacon Soup
½ cup sour cream
1 teaspoon chili powder
½ cup PACE Thick & Chunky Salsa
1 cup shredded Cheddar cheese (4 ounces)
    Sliced green onions
    Sliced VLASIC *or* EARLY CALIFORNIA pitted
    Ripe Olives
1 bag (about 10 ounces) tortilla chips

• In small bowl, combine soup, sour cream and chili powder. Spread on 10-inch plate. Top with salsa, cheese, onions and olives. Serve with tortilla chips for dipping. If desired, garnish with *pitted ripe olives* and *fresh cilantro*.

MAKES ABOUT 1½ CUPS
PREP TIME: 20 MINUTES

Orange Mist

1 can (46 ounces) V8 Vegetable Juice
1 can (6 ounces) frozen orange juice concentrate
1½ cups seltzer water *or* orange-flavored seltzer water

• In large pitcher, combine "V8" juice and orange juice.

• Stir in seltzer water. Pour immediately over ice. If desired, garnish with *orange* and *celery*.

MAKES ABOUT 7½ CUPS OR 10 SERVINGS
PREP TIME: 5 MINUTES

Mexicali Dip

Whatever the occasion, guests love to take a dip at a party! This zesty dip with a spicy accent also makes a splash when served warm. Just spread mixture onto a microwave-safe plate and top with remaining ingredients. Microwave on HIGH power for 2 minutes. Serve with tortilla chips and watch your guests dive in!

TANGY BAKED WINGS

1 pouch CAMPBELL'S Dry Onion with Chicken Broth Soup and Recipe Mix
⅓ cup honey
2 tablespoons spicy brown mustard
18 chicken wings (about 3 pounds)

• In large bowl, combine soup mix, honey and mustard; set aside.

• Cut tips off wings; discard tips or save for another use. Cut wings in half at joints to make 36 pieces. Add to soup mixture; toss to coat.

• In large shallow baking pan, arrange wings. Bake at 400°F. for 25 minutes. Turn wings. Bake 20 minutes more or until wings are no longer pink. If desired, garnish with *celery*.

MAKES 36 APPETIZERS
PREP TIME: 15 MINUTES   COOK TIME: 45 MINUTES

CRAB DIP

1 cup refrigerated MARIE'S Creamy Ranch Dressing and Dip
1 can (about 6 ounces) white crab meat, drained
2 green onions, sliced (about ¼ cup)
1 teaspoon lemon juice
  Dash hot pepper sauce
  PEPPERIDGE FARM Crackers *and/or* assorted fresh vegetables

• In small bowl, combine dressing, crab, onions, lemon juice and hot pepper sauce. Cover; refrigerate at least 1 hour before serving. Serve with crackers or vegetables for dipping. If desired, garnish with *green onion* and *lemon peel*.

MAKES ABOUT 1½ CUPS
PREP TIME: 10 MINUTES   CHILL TIME: 1 HOUR

Your "game plan" for clean-up will be easier if you bake the wings in a foil-lined pan. Don't be surprised if these tasty wings "fly" off the serving dish and onto the plates of your guests almost as soon as you put them on the table. Play it safe and make an extra batch!

Tangy Baked Wings (*left*)
Crab Dip (*right*)

CRUNCHY CHICKEN NIBBLES

1½ pounds skinless, boneless chicken breasts, cut into 1-inch pieces
  1 jar (12 ounces) refrigerated MARIE'S Honey Mustard Dressing and Dip
  2 cups PEPPERIDGE FARM Herb Seasoned Stuffing, crushed
  2 tablespoons orange juice

• In shallow dish, dip chicken into *¾ cup* dressing. On waxed paper, coat chicken with stuffing.

• On baking sheet, arrange chicken. Bake at 400°F. for 15 minutes or until chicken is no longer pink.

• In 1-quart saucepan, combine remaining dressing and orange juice. Over medium heat, heat through, stirring occasionally. Serve with chicken for dipping.

MAKES ABOUT 40 APPETIZERS
PREP TIME: 15 MINUTES   COOK TIME: 15 MINUTES

KIDS' HALLOWEEN SUPPER

Crunchy
Chicken
Nibbles
•
Fruit kabobs
•
Celery and
carrot sticks
•
Snack mix
•
Jack-O'-Lantern
Cupcakes
(p. 26)
•
Cider

Jack-O'-Lantern Cupcakes *(top, recipe page 26)*
Crunchy Chicken Nibbles *(bottom)*

VEGETABLE TORTILLA BITES

1 **pouch CAMPBELL'S Dry Onion Soup and Recipe Mix**
1 **package (8 ounces) cream cheese, softened**
1 **small carrot, shredded (about ¼ cup)**
2 **green onions, chopped (about ¼ cup)**
1 **teaspoon Louisiana-style hot sauce**
6 **flour tortillas (8 inches *each*)**

• In small bowl, combine soup mix and cream cheese until smooth. Add carrot, onions and hot sauce. Spread each tortilla with about ¼ *cup* cheese mixture, spreading evenly to edge.

• Tightly roll up, jelly-roll fashion; place seam-side down in large shallow dish. Cover; refrigerate at least 2 hours before serving.

• Trim ends of tortilla roll-ups. Cut each roll-up into 1-inch slices. If desired, garnish with *jalapeño peppers, carrot* and *green onion*.

MAKES ABOUT 36 APPETIZERS
PREP TIME: 20 MINUTES   CHILL TIME: 2 HOURS

It's a snap to soften cream cheese in the microwave. Remove packaging, place on microwave-safe dish and microwave 8 ounces of cheese at 50% power (medium) for 1 to 1½ minutes.

Pizza is always

a winning

ingredient for

satisfying hungry

squads of

armchair

quarterbacks.

Your home team

and visitors will

stand up and

cheer this quick

and easy crowd-

pleaser!

MUSTARD-ONION DIP

1 pouch CAMPBELL'S Dry Onion Soup and Recipe Mix
1 container (16 ounces) sour cream
1 tablespoon spicy brown mustard
1 tablespoon honey
   PEPPERIDGE FARM Crackers, pretzels *and/or* assorted fresh vegetables

• In bowl, mix soup mix, sour cream, mustard and honey. Cover; refrigerate at least 2 hours before serving. Serve with crackers, pretzels or fresh vegetables for dipping. If desired, garnish with *radishes* and *fresh dill.*

MAKES ABOUT 2 CUPS
PREP TIME: 5 MINUTES   CHILL TIME: 2 HOURS

SOUPER MUSHROOM PIZZA

1 loaf (about 14 ounces) Italian bread
1 can (10¾ ounces) CAMPBELL'S condensed Cream of Mushroom Soup
1 cup shredded mozzarella cheese (4 ounces)
1 small sweet red pepper, chopped (about ½ cup)
2 green onions, chopped (about ¼ cup)
1 tablespoon grated Parmesan cheese
¼ teaspoon garlic powder
¼ teaspoon Italian seasoning, crushed

• Cut bread in half lengthwise. Place on baking sheet. Bake at 400°F. for 10 minutes or until lightly toasted.

• In bowl, mix remaining ingredients; spread on bread. Bake 5 minutes more or until cheese is melted. Cut each bread half into 12 slices.

MAKES 24 APPETIZERS
PREP TIME: 15 MINUTES   COOK TIME: 15 MINUTES

NACHOS GRANDE

1 can (10¾ ounces) **CAMPBELL'S condensed Cheddar Cheese Soup**
½ cup **PACE Thick & Chunky Salsa**
1 pound **ground beef**
1 small **onion, chopped (about ¼ cup)**
5 cups **tortilla chips (about 5 ounces)**
1 medium **tomato, chopped (about 1 cup)**
1 **fresh jalapeño pepper, sliced (optional)**

• In 1-quart saucepan, combine soup and salsa; set aside.

• In 10-inch skillet over medium-high heat, cook beef and onion until beef is browned and onion is tender, stirring to separate meat. Spoon off fat. Add *½ cup* soup mixture. Reduce heat to medium. Heat through, stirring occasionally.

• Over medium heat, heat remaining soup mixture, stirring occasionally.

• Arrange chips on large serving platter; top with meat mixture. Spoon soup mixture over meat. Top with tomato and pepper. If desired, garnish with *fresh cilantro*.

MAKES ABOUT 2 CUPS OR 8 APPETIZER SERVINGS
PREP TIME: 10 MINUTES   COOK TIME: 10 MINUTES

Why wear rubber gloves when handling jalapeño peppers? It's a burning question! Jalapeños contain oils that can cause a stinging sensation on your skin.

SPORTS LOVERS TAILGATE

ZESTY ANTIPASTO

½ cup refrigerated **MARIE'S Zesty Fat Free Italian Vinaigrette**
 1 jar (22 ounces) **VLASIC Pepperoncini Salad Peppers**, drained
 1 can (6 ounces) **VLASIC** *or* **EARLY CALIFORNIA** pitted large Ripe Olives,
   drained
 8 ounces provolone cheese, cut into cubes
 2 cups fresh mushrooms cut in half (about 6 ounces)
 2 cups cherry tomatoes cut in half
 4 ounces pepperoni, sliced
   Lettuce leaves

• In large, shallow nonmetallic dish, pour vinaigrette. Add peppers, olives, cheese, mushrooms, tomatoes and pepperoni; toss to coat. Cover; refrigerate at least 30 minutes before serving.

• Spoon onto lettuce. Serve with toothpicks.

MAKES ABOUT 8 CUPS OR 16 APPETIZER SERVINGS
PREP TIME: 20 MINUTES   CHILL TIME: 30 MINUTES

TOMATO-ZUCCHINI BREAD

3 cups all-purpose flour

2 teaspoons ground cinnamon

1 teaspoon baking soda

½ teaspoon baking powder

1½ cups sugar

1 can (10¾ ounces) **CAMPBELL'S HEALTHY REQUEST**
   condensed Tomato Soup

6 egg whites

⅓ cup vegetable oil

1 teaspoon vanilla extract

2 cups shredded zucchini (about 2 small)

1 cup raisins

• Preheat oven to 350°F. Grease two 8½- by 4½-inch loaf pans; set aside.

• In large bowl, combine flour, cinnamon, baking soda and baking powder; set aside.

• In medium bowl, combine sugar, soup, egg whites, oil and vanilla. Stir soup mixture into flour mixture just until blended. Fold in zucchini and raisins. Pour into prepared pans.

• Bake in center of oven 55 minutes or until toothpick inserted in center comes out clean. Cool in pans on wire rack 10 minutes. Remove from pans; cool completely on rack. If desired, garnish with *fresh mint* and *orange peel*.

MAKES 2 LOAVES (12 SERVINGS *EACH*)
PREP TIME: 20 MINUTES   COOK TIME: 55 MINUTES

Mini Loaves: Pour batter evenly into four greased 5¾- by 3¼-inch mini loaf pans instead of two 8½- by 4½-inch loaf pans. Bake 45 minutes or until toothpick inserted in center comes out clean. Cool. Makes 4 loaves (6 servings *each*).

Here's a great way to "share" this recipe with a friend. Nestle a wooden spoon into a loaf pan along with a pot holder, box of raisins, small container of ground cinnamon and a can of Campbell's Healthy Request condensed Tomato Soup. Wrap in a festive kitchen towel with the printed recipe tucked inside and give as a housewarming or hostess gift.

Easy Apple Crisp

1 can (21 ounces) apple pie filling
2 **PEPPERIDGE FARM AMERICAN COLLECTION** Santa Fe Oatmeal Raisin
 or Soft Baked Oatmeal Raisin Cookies, coarsely crumbled (about 1 cup)
½ cup chopped walnuts (optional)
2 tablespoons margarine *or* butter, melted
 Ice cream *or* frozen yogurt

• Spoon pie filling into 1-quart casserole.

• In small bowl, combine cookies, walnuts and margarine. Sprinkle over filling. Bake at 400°F. for 15 minutes or until warm. Serve with ice cream or frozen yogurt. If desired, garnish with *fresh mint.*

MAKES ABOUT 3 CUPS OR 6 SERVINGS
PREP TIME: 10 MINUTES COOK TIME: 15 MINUTES

This all-American dessert is ready when you are. Assemble the ingredients before guests arrive, then pop it in the oven right before you sit down to enjoy your main course.

HOLIDAY SPICE CAKE

Holidays have a special flavor and feeling all their own. This classic Campbell's recipe has remained popular through generations because it engagingly wraps some of the holiday season's traditional flavors around the spirit of friendship and giving.

Portable *Holiday Spice Cake* is ideal to take to your next office party, potluck or tailgate.

   2 cups all-purpose flour
1⅓ cups sugar
   4 teaspoons baking powder
1½ teaspoons ground allspice
   1 teaspoon baking soda
   1 teaspoon ground cinnamon
   ½ teaspoon ground cloves
   1 can (10¾ ounces) **CAMPBELL'S** condensed Tomato Soup
   ½ cup vegetable shortening
   2 eggs
   ¼ cup water

• Preheat oven to 350°F. Grease and lightly flour 13- by 9-inch baking pan; set aside.

• In mixer bowl, combine first 7 ingredients. Add soup, shortening, eggs and water. Beat at low speed until well mixed, constantly scraping bowl. At high speed, beat 4 minutes, scraping bowl often. Pour into prepared pan.

• Bake 40 minutes or until toothpick inserted in center comes out clean. Cool in pan on wire rack 10 minutes. Remove; cool completely. Frost with *cream cheese frosting*. If desired, garnish with *candied orange peel*, *cinnamon* and *edible flowers*.

MAKES 12 SERVINGS	
PREP TIME: 20 MINUTES	BAKE & COOL TIME: 3 HOURS

Jack-O'-Lantern Cupcakes: Place liners in twenty-four 3-inch muffin cups. Spoon batter into cups. Bake 30 minutes. Remove from pans; cool. Frost. If desired, decorate with *candy*. Makes 24.

Holiday Spice Ring: Pour batter into greased and floured 10-inch fluted tube pan. Bake 1 hour. Drizzle with *vanilla glaze*. If desired, garnish with *fruit* and *fresh mint*.

Easy Fruit Shells

1 package (10 ounces) PEPPERIDGE FARM Frozen Puff Pastry Shells
1 package (about 3½ ounces) vanilla instant pudding mix
2 cups milk
2 cups cut-up fresh fruit
   Whipped topping *or* whipped cream

• Prepare pastry shells according to package directions; cool completely.

• Prepare pudding according to package directions.

• Spoon about *⅓ cup* pudding into each pastry shell. Divide fruit evenly among pastry shells. Top with whipped topping. Serve immediately or cover and refrigerate up to 4 hours before serving. If desired, garnish with *fresh mint*.

Makes 6 servings	Prep Time: 50 minutes

Come For Dessert

Easy Fruit
Shells
•
Godiva Coffees
•
Herbal teas
•
Godiva
Chocolates

Fast & Festive Skillets

You don't have to wait for the Chinese New Year to serve popular *Sweet-and-Sour Chicken,* a colorful and classy main dish that will suit your hectic holiday or weekday schedule year 'round! Simply sophisticated *Lemony Olive Chicken* and these other delicious skillet sensations create menu magic in minutes!

Sweet-and-Sour Chicken (page 32) and *Lemony Olive Chicken (page 33).*

SWEET-AND-SOUR CHICKEN

3 tablespoons cornstarch

1 can (10½ ounces) CAMPBELL'S condensed Chicken Broth

1 tablespoon vegetable oil

1 pound skinless, boneless chicken breasts, cut into 1-inch pieces

1 can (8 ounces) pineapple chunks in juice, undrained

1 medium green *or* sweet red pepper, cut into strips (about 1 cup)

¼ cup sugar

¼ cup vinegar

4 cups hot cooked rice

• In cup, stir together cornstarch and broth until smooth; set aside.

• In 10-inch skillet over medium-high heat, in hot oil, stir-fry *half* of the chicken until browned. Remove; set aside. Repeat with remaining chicken. Pour off fat.

• Reduce heat to medium. In same skillet, combine *undrained* pineapple, pepper, sugar, vinegar and reserved cornstarch mixture. Cook until mixture boils and thickens, stirring constantly. Return chicken to skillet. Reduce heat to low. Cover; cook 5 minutes or until pepper is tender, stirring occasionally. Serve over rice. If desired, garnish with *strawberries* and *fresh pineapple leaves*.

MAKES ABOUT 4 CUPS OR 4 SERVINGS
PREP TIME: 15 MINUTES   COOK TIME: 20 MINUTES

EASY CHINESE NEW YEAR

Won Ton soup

•

Sweet-and-
Sour Chicken

•

Rice

•

Broccoli

•

Almond
cookies,
orange wedges
and sorbet

LEMONY OLIVE CHICKEN

1 tablespoon vegetable oil
4 skinless, boneless chicken breast halves (about 1 pound)
1 can (10¾ ounces) **CAMPBELL'S** condensed Cream of Chicken Soup
¼ cup milk
½ teaspoon lemon juice
⅛ teaspoon pepper
½ cup sliced **VLASIC** *or* **EARLY CALIFORNIA** pitted Ripe Olives
4 thin lemon slices
4 cups hot cooked rice

• In 10-inch skillet over medium-high heat, in hot oil, cook chicken 10 minutes or until browned on both sides. Remove; set aside. Pour off fat.

• In same skillet, combine soup, milk, juice and pepper; add olives. Heat to boiling. Return chicken to skillet; top with lemon slices. Reduce heat to low. Cover; cook 5 minutes or until chicken is no longer pink. Serve with rice. If desired, garnish with *fresh mint*.

MAKES 4 SERVINGS
PREP TIME: 10 MINUTES   COOK TIME: 20 MINUTES

LEMONY OLIVE
CHICKEN

When shopping for skinless, boneless chicken breasts, the chicken meat should be light in color, not gray or pasty looking. Look for a "sell by" label on the package. Most chicken processors specify the last day poultry should be sold. Avoid packages with expired dates.

BASIL CHICKEN 'N' VEGETABLES

1 tablespoon vegetable oil

4 skinless, boneless chicken breast halves (about 1 pound)

1 can (10¾ ounces) CAMPBELL'S condensed Cream of Broccoli Soup

½ cup milk

¼ teaspoon dried basil leaves, crushed

⅛ teaspoon pepper

1 bag (16 ounces) frozen vegetable combination
   (broccoli, cauliflower and carrots)

• In 10-inch skillet over medium-high heat, in hot oil, cook chicken 10 minutes or until browned on both sides. Remove; set aside. Pour off fat.

• In same skillet, combine soup, milk, basil and pepper; add vegetables. Heat to boiling. Return chicken to skillet. Reduce heat to low. Cover; cook 10 minutes or until chicken is no longer pink and vegetables are tender, stirring occasionally. If desired, garnish with *fresh herbs*.

MAKES 4 SERVINGS
PREP TIME: 5 MINUTES   COOK TIME: 25 MINUTES

RUSH-HOUR SUPPER

Basil Chicken 'n' Vegetables

•

Fruit salad

•

Bread sticks

•

Raspberry sherbet and cookies

Easy Chicken Stroganoff

LIGHT & EASY SUPPER

Easy Chicken
Stroganoff

•

Salad

•

Rolls

•

Fresh fruit
medley

2   tablespoons vegetable oil
1   pound skinless, boneless chicken breasts, cut into strips
2   cups sliced fresh mushrooms (about 6 ounces)
1   medium onion, chopped (about ½ cup)
1   can (10¾ ounces) CAMPBELL'S HEALTHY REQUEST
     condensed Cream of Chicken Soup
½   cup plain nonfat yogurt
¼   cup water
4   cups hot cooked egg noodles
     (about 4 cups dry)
    Paprika

• In 10-inch skillet over medium-high heat, in *1 tablespoon* hot oil, cook *half* of the chicken until browned, stirring often. Remove; set aside. Repeat with remaining chicken.

• Reduce heat to medium. In same skillet, in remaining *1 tablespoon* hot oil, cook mushrooms and onion until tender and liquid is evaporated, stirring often.

• Stir in soup, yogurt and water. Heat to boiling. Return chicken to skillet. Heat through, stirring occasionally. Serve over noodles. Sprinkle with paprika. If desired, garnish with *celery leaves, sweet red pepper* and *red onion*.

MAKES 4 SERVINGS
PREP TIME: 15 MINUTES   COOK TIME: 25 MINUTES

SHOPPING
SURVIVAL
SUPPER

Chicken
Primavera
•
Romaine salad
•
Italian bread
•
Lemon mousse
cake

CHICKEN PRIMAVERA

2 tablespoons margarine *or* butter

2 cups fresh broccoli flowerets

2 medium carrots, sliced (about 1 cup)

1 can (19 ounces) **CAMPBELL'S HOME COOKIN'** Ready To Serve
   Cream of Mushroom Soup

2 cups cubed cooked chicken

2 tablespoons grated Parmesan cheese

⅛ teaspoon pepper

4 cups hot cooked spaghetti *or* fettuccine
   (about 8 ounces dry)

• In 10-inch skillet over medium heat, in hot margarine, cook broccoli and carrots until tender-crisp, stirring often. Add soup, chicken, cheese and pepper. Heat through, stirring occasionally. Serve over spaghetti. If desired, garnish with *fresh tarragon* and *sweet red pepper*.

MAKES 4 SERVINGS
PREP TIME: 15 MINUTES   COOK TIME: 10 MINUTES

Shortcut Chicken Cordon Bleu

1 tablespoon margarine *or* butter

4 skinless, boneless chicken breast halves (about 1 pound)

1 can (10¾ ounces) CAMPBELL'S condensed Cream of Chicken Soup

½ cup shredded Swiss cheese (2 ounces)

½ cup chopped cooked ham

¼ cup water *or* dry white wine

4 cups hot cooked egg noodles (about 4 cups dry)

• In 10-inch skillet over medium-high heat, in hot margarine, cook chicken 10 minutes or until browned on both sides. Remove; set aside.

• In same skillet, combine soup, cheese, ham and water. Heat to boiling, stirring often. Return chicken to skillet. Reduce heat to low. Cover; cook 5 minutes or until chicken is no longer pink, stirring occasionally. Serve with noodles. If desired, garnish with *carrot curl*.

MAKES 4 SERVINGS

PREP TIME: 10 MINUTES   COOK TIME: 20 MINUTES

COMPANY'S COMING IN 30 MINUTES!

Cheese and crackers

•

Shortcut Chicken Cordon Bleu

•

Salad

•

Sugar snap peas

•

Easy Apple Crisp (p. 24)

BEEF AND MUSHROOMS DIJON

1 pound boneless beef sirloin *or* top round steak, ¾ inch thick
2 tablespoons vegetable oil
2 cups sliced fresh mushrooms (about 6 ounces)
1 medium onion, sliced (about ½ cup)
1 can (10¾ ounces) CAMPBELL'S condensed Cream of Mushroom Soup
½ cup water
2 tablespoons Dijon-style mustard
4 cups hot cooked rice

• Slice beef across the grain into thin strips.

• In 10-inch skillet over medium-high heat, in *1 tablespoon* hot oil, cook *half* of the beef until browned, stirring often. Remove; set aside. Repeat with remaining beef.

• Reduce heat to medium. In same skillet, in remaining *1 tablespoon* hot oil, cook mushrooms and onion until tender and liquid is evaporated, stirring often.

• Stir in soup, water and mustard. Heat to boiling. Return beef to skillet. Heat through, stirring occasionally. Serve over rice. If desired, garnish with *fresh chives.*

MAKES 4 SERVINGS
PREP TIME: 15 MINUTES   COOK TIME: 25 MINUTES

BEEF AND
MUSHROOMS DIJON

You've got enough to do — and not nearly enough time to do it! With hearty, palate-pleasing dishes like this one, you can let Campbell's put the "skill" in your skillet dinner. So sit back and bask in the compliments of a very satisfied crowd that's sure you spent hours preparing their dinner.

AUTUMN PORK CHOPS

Remember to
start the water for
the noodles as
you begin
cooking the pork
chops.

Prepared
mustards are
made from the
tiny seeds of the
mustard plant.
The seeds are
first dried, then
ground into paste
with water,
vinegar or wine.
Generally, the
yellower the
mustard, the
milder the taste
or pungency.

AUTUMN PORK CHOPS

1 tablespoon vegetable oil
4 pork chops, each ¾ inch thick (about 1½ lbs.)
1 can (10¾ ounces) CAMPBELL'S condensed Cream of Celery Soup
½ cup apple juice *or* water
2 tablespoons spicy brown mustard
1 tablespoon honey
   Generous dash pepper
4 cups hot cooked egg noodles (about 4 cups dry)

• In skillet over medium-high heat, in hot oil, cook chops 10 minutes or until browned. Remove. Pour off fat. In same pan, heat next 5 ingredients to boiling. Add chops. Reduce heat to low. Cover; cook 10 minutes or until done. Serve with noodles. If desired, garnish with *apple* and *fresh herbs*.

MAKES 4 SERVINGS
PREP TIME: 5 MINUTES   COOK TIME: 25 MINUTES

COUNTRY SKILLET CHOPS

½ teaspoon garlic powder
¼ teaspoon pepper
6 pork chops, each ¾ inch thick (about 2 lbs.)
1 tablespoon olive *or* vegetable oil
1 can (19 ounces) CAMPBELL'S HOME COOKIN' Ready to Serve
   Cream of Mushroom Soup
6 cups hot cooked egg noodles (about 6 cups dry)

• Sprinkle garlic powder and pepper on both sides of chops.

• In skillet over medium-high heat, in hot oil, cook *half* of the chops 10 minutes or until browned. Remove. Repeat with remaining chops. Pour off fat. In same pan, stir soup and heat to boiling. Return chops to pan. Reduce heat to low. Cover; cook 10 minutes or until done. Serve with noodles.

MAKES 6 SERVINGS
PREP TIME: 5 MINUTES   COOK TIME: 35 MINUTES

Shrimp and Broccoli

1 tablespoon olive *or* vegetable oil

2 cups fresh broccoli flowerets

¼ teaspoon garlic powder *or* 2 cloves garlic, minced

1 can (10¾ ounces) CAMPBELL'S condensed Cream of Broccoli Soup

½ cup water

1 pound medium shrimp, shelled and deveined

1 tablespoon lemon juice

⅛ teaspoon pepper

2 packages (3 ounces *each*) CAMPBELL'S *or* SANWA RAMEN PRIDE Chicken
Flavor Ramen Noodle Soup *or* 4 cups hot cooked rice

• In 10-inch skillet over medium heat, in hot oil, cook broccoli with garlic powder until tender-crisp, stirring often.

• Stir in broccoli soup and water. Heat to boiling. Add shrimp, lemon juice and pepper. Cook 5 minutes or until shrimp turn pink and opaque, stirring often. Serve over noodles. If desired, garnish with *lemon* and *fresh mint.*

MAKES ABOUT 4 CUPS OR 4 SERVINGS
PREP TIME: 20 MINUTES   COOK TIME: 15 MINUTES

When purchasing fresh shrimp, keep in mind that about 1¼ pounds of shrimp in shells will yield about 1 pound shelled, deveined shrimp.

SKIP-A-STEP OVEN SUPPERS

See for yourself how skipping a step can keep the festivities hopping! *Turkey-Broccoli Divan* and *Chicken Enchiladas* transform leftovers into new and exciting main dishes for lunch, brunch or dinner. Streamlined for a potluck buffet or informal gathering, *Easy Party Lasagna* and *Ranchero Macaroni Bake* are also great for satisfying your favorite tree trimmers!

Chicken Enchiladas (page 51)
and Turkey-Broccoli Divan (page 50).

TURKEY-BROCCOLI DIVAN

TURKEY-BROCCOLI
DIVAN

A simply *divan*
way to use leftover
chicken or turkey!
Or, substitute two
5-ounce cans of
Swanson Chunk
Turkey *or* Chicken,
drained.

1 **pound fresh broccoli, cut into flowerets**
    (about 4 cups), cooked and drained
1½ **cups cubed cooked turkey *or* chicken**
1 **can (10¾ ounces) CAMPBELL'S condensed Broccoli Cheese Soup**
⅓ **cup milk**
½ **cup shredded Cheddar cheese (optional)**
2 **tablespoons dry bread crumbs**
1 **tablespoon margarine *or* butter, melted**

• In 9-inch pie plate or 2-quart oblong baking dish, arrange broccoli and
turkey. In bowl, combine soup and milk; pour over broccoli and turkey.

• Sprinkle cheese over soup mixture. In cup, combine bread crumbs and
margarine; sprinkle over cheese.

• Bake at 450°F. for 20 minutes or until hot and bubbling. If desired, garnish
with *fresh kale leaves.*

MAKES 4 SERVINGS

PREP TIME: 15 MINUTES   COOK TIME: 20 MINUTES

CHICKEN ENCHILADAS

1 can (10¾ ounces) CAMPBELL'S condensed Cream of Chicken Soup
½ cup sour cream
2 tablespoons margarine *or* butter
1 medium onion, chopped (about ½ cup)
1 teaspoon chili powder
2 cups chopped cooked chicken *or* turkey
1 can (4 ounces) chopped green chilies
8 flour tortillas (8 inches *each*)
1 cup shredded Cheddar *or* Monterey Jack cheese (4 ounces)

• In small bowl, combine soup and sour cream; set aside.

• In 2-quart saucepan over medium heat, in hot margarine, cook onion and chili powder until tender, stirring often. Stir in chicken, chilies and *2 tablespoons* soup mixture. Remove from heat.

• Spread *½ cup* soup mixture in 2-quart oblong baking dish. Along one side of each tortilla, spread about *¼ cup* chicken mixture. Roll up each tortilla around filling and place seam-side down in baking dish.

• Spread remaining soup mixture over enchiladas. Sprinkle cheese over soup mixture. Bake at 350°F. for 25 minutes or until hot and bubbling. If desired, garnish with *radishes, olives, shredded lettuce* and *lime*.

MAKES 4 SERVINGS
PREP TIME: 25 MINUTES   COOK TIME: 25 MINUTES

Entertaining a group of thrill-seekers? Substitute Monterey Jack cheese with jalapeño peppers for Cheddar or Monterey Jack cheese. And, have plenty of glasses of ice-cold water nearby to put out the fire!

To reduce fat, remove skin from the chicken before baking.

Selecting the freshest mushrooms is a beauty contest, so choose only the most attractive. The caps should be firm, bright and bruise-free. The grills underneath the cap should be lightly closed.

CHICKEN AND RICE BAKE

1 can (10¾ ounces) **CAMPBELL'S** condensed
    Cream of Chicken & Broccoli Soup
1½ cups water
1½ cups sliced fresh mushrooms (about 4 ounces)
¾ cup uncooked regular long-grain rice
1 can (2.8 ounces) French fried onions
4 chicken breast halves (about 2 pounds)
    Paprika
    Pepper

• In 3-quart oblong baking dish, combine soup, water, mushrooms, rice and *half* of onions. Arrange chicken on rice mixture; sprinkle with paprika and pepper.

• Bake at 375°F. for 1 hour or until chicken is no longer pink. Sprinkle remaining onions over chicken mixture.

• Bake 3 minutes more or until onions are golden. If desired, garnish with *zucchini* and *fresh thyme*.

MAKES 4 SERVINGS
PREP TIME: 10 MINUTES   COOK TIME: 1 HOUR 3 MINUTES

EASY PARTY LASAGNA

1 **pound ground beef**
1 **can (11⅛ ounces) CAMPBELL'S condensed Italian Tomato Soup**
1 **cup water**
1 **can (10¾ ounces) CAMPBELL'S condensed Cream of Mushroom Soup**
2 **cups shredded mozzarella cheese (8 ounces)**
¼ **cup milk**
6 *dry* **lasagna noodles**

• In 10-inch skillet over medium-high heat, cook beef until browned, stirring to separate meat. Spoon off fat. Add tomato soup and water. Heat through, stirring occasionally. Remove from heat.

• In small bowl, combine mushroom soup, *½ cup* cheese and milk.

• In 2-quart oblong baking dish, spoon *half* the meat mixture. Top with *3* lasagna noodles. Spoon mushroom soup mixture over lasagna noodles. Top with remaining *3* lasagna noodles and remaining meat mixture. Cover tightly with foil.

• Bake at 400°F. for 40 minutes. Uncover; sprinkle remaining *1½ cups* cheese over meat mixture. Bake 10 minutes more or until hot and bubbling. Let stand 10 minutes before serving. If desired, garnish with *tomato, fresh basil, bay leaves* and *Parmesan cheese.*

MAKES 8 SERVINGS		
PREP TIME: 15 MINUTES	COOK TIME: 50 MINUTES	STAND TIME: 10 MINUTES

POTLUCK DINNER

Zesty Antipasto
(p. 20)

•

Easy Party
Lasagna

•

Garlic bread

•

Ranch Layered
Salad (p. 74)

•

Cheesecake

ITALIAN MEAT LOAF

1 can (11⅛ ounces) **CAMPBELL'S condensed Italian Tomato Soup**
1½ **pounds ground beef**
½ **cup Italian-seasoned dry bread crumbs**
1 **tablespoon Worcestershire sauce**
1 **egg, beaten**
⅛ **teaspoon pepper**
¼ **cup water**

• In large bowl, mix *thoroughly* ½ *cup* soup, beef, bread crumbs, Worcestershire sauce, egg and pepper. In 2-quart oblong baking dish, *firmly* shape meat mixture into 8- by 4-inch loaf.

• Bake at 350°F. for 1 hour or until meat loaf is no longer pink (160°F. internal temperature). Reserve 2 tablespoons drippings.

• In 1-quart saucepan over medium heat, combine remaining soup, water and reserved drippings. Heat through, stirring occasionally. Serve with meat loaf. If desired, garnish with *baby corn, zucchini, tomatoes* and *fresh sage.*

MAKES 6 SERVINGS
PREP TIME: 15 MINUTES   COOK TIME: 1 HOUR 5 MINUTES

It's not a rock star on a European tour...it's everybody's favorite comfort food classic with the unmistakable seasonings and aroma of Roma! Not to be confused with other robust imitators, *this* meat loaf sings in its own savory sauce — no other gravy or condiment accompaniment necessary. Mangia!

❖

HANUKKAH CELEBRATION

Savory Beef
Roast

•

Potato latkes

•

Poached apples

•

Salad

•

Noodle kugel

SAVORY BEEF ROAST

  2 tablespoons vegetable oil

3½- to 4-pound boneless beef bottom round *or* chuck pot roast

  1 can (10¾ ounces) CAMPBELL'S condensed Cream of Mushroom Soup

  1 pouch CAMPBELL'S Dry Onion Soup and Recipe Mix

  1 teaspoon dried thyme leaves, crushed

  1 bay leaf

1¼ cups water

  8 medium potatoes, cut into quarters (about 7 cups)

  8 medium carrots, cut into 2-inch pieces (about 4 cups)

  2 tablespoons all-purpose flour

• In 6-quart oven-safe Dutch oven over medium-high heat, in hot oil, cook roast until browned on all sides. Remove; set aside. Pour off fat.

• In same Dutch oven, combine mushroom soup, soup mix, thyme, bay leaf and *1 cup* water. Return roast to Dutch oven. Cover; bake at 350°F. for 45 minutes.

• Turn roast; add potatoes and carrots. Cover; bake 1 hour 45 minutes or until roast and vegetables are fork-tender.

• Transfer roast and vegetables to platter. In cup, stir together flour and remaining *¼ cup* water until smooth. Gradually stir into soup mixture. Over medium heat, cook until mixture boils and thickens, stirring constantly. Discard bay leaf. Serve gravy with roast and vegetables. If desired, garnish with *fresh thyme.*

MAKES 8 SERVINGS

PREP TIME: 10 MINUTES   COOK TIME: 2 HOURS 45 MINUTES

RANCHERO MACARONI BAKE

1 can (26 ounces) CAMPBELL'S condensed Cream of Chicken Soup
1 cup milk
6 cups hot cooked elbow macaroni (about 3 cups dry)
3 cups shredded Cheddar *or* Monterey Jack cheese (12 ounces)
1 cup PACE Thick & Chunky Salsa
1 cup coarsely crushed tortilla chips

• In large bowl, combine soup and milk. Stir in macaroni, cheese and salsa. Spoon into 3-quart oblong baking dish.

• Bake at 400°F. for 20 minutes; stir. Sprinkle chips over macaroni mixture.

• Bake 5 minutes more or until hot and bubbling. If desired, garnish with *fresh chili pepper* and *fresh cilantro*.

MAKES ABOUT 12 CUPS OR 8 MAIN-DISH SERVINGS
PREP TIME: 20 MINUTES   COOK TIME: 25 MINUTES

TRIM-A-TREE FIESTA

Pace Salsa, guacamole and chips

•

Ranchero Macaroni Bake

•

Spinach and orange salad

•

Zucchini

•

Lemon sherbet and cookies

EASY-ON-YOU HOLIDAY BRUNCH

Tomato and orange juice

•

Cheddar-Swiss Strata

•

Sausage

•

Blueberry muffins

•

Tomato-Zucchini Bread (p. 22)

•

Medley of fresh fruit

•

Coffee and tea

CHEDDAR-SWISS STRATA

6 cups French *or* Italian bread cut in 1-inch cubes
1 can (10¾ ounces) CAMPBELL'S condensed Cheddar Cheese Soup
1 cup milk
4 eggs, beaten
1½ cups shredded Swiss cheese (6 ounces)

• In greased 2-quart oblong baking dish, arrange bread cubes. In medium bowl, combine soup, milk and eggs. Stir in cheese. Pour over bread. Cover; refrigerate overnight.

• Uncover; bake at 350°F. for 40 minutes or until set. If desired, garnish with *fresh herbs.*

MAKES 8 SERVINGS
PREP TIME: 15 MINUTES   COOK TIME: 40 MINUTES

SIMPLY
SAVORY
SIDES

Whether it's a holiday turkey, roast or ham, no "Big Day" dinner would be completely dressed without a spectacular side dish or salad! Scrumptious accompaniments like *Swiss Vegetable Bake, Fiesta Potatoes, Souper Rice* and *Ranch Layered Salad* deliver distinctive seasonings and variety to your holiday table — and excitement to just about everything else you're serving!

Swiss Vegetable Bake (page 67) and
Cheddar-Potato Bake (page 66).

&❧

THE "BIG DAY" DINNER

Roast turkey,
stuffing and
gravy
•
Swiss Vegetable
Bake (p. 67)
•
Cheddar-Potato
Bake
•
Ginger-
Cranberry
Sauce
(p. 67)
•
Relish tray
•
Rolls
•
Pumpkin pie
•
Coffee

CHEDDAR-POTATO BAKE

1 can (10¾ ounces) **CAMPBELL'S** condensed Cheddar Cheese Soup
⅓ cup sour cream *or* plain yogurt
1 green onion, chopped (about 2 tablespoons)
   Generous dash pepper
3 cups stiff, seasoned mashed potatoes
2 tablespoons dry bread crumbs
1 tablespoon margarine *or* butter, melted
¼ teaspoon paprika

• In 1½-quart casserole, combine soup, sour cream, onion and pepper. Stir in potatoes.

• In cup, combine bread crumbs, margarine and paprika. Sprinkle over potato mixture. Bake at 350°F. for 30 minutes or until hot. If desired, garnish with *Brussels sprouts* and *fresh thyme*.

MAKES ABOUT 4 CUPS OR 8 SERVINGS
PREP TIME: 10 MINUTES   COOK TIME: 30 MINUTES

Swiss Vegetable Bake

1 can (26 ounces) CAMPBELL'S condensed Cream of Chicken Soup
⅔ cup sour cream
½ teaspoon pepper
2 bags (16 ounces *each*) frozen vegetable combination
    (broccoli, cauliflower and carrots), thawed
2 cups shredded Swiss cheese (8 ounces)
1 can (6 ounces) *or* 2 cans (2.8 ounces *each*) French fried onions

• In large bowl, combine soup, sour cream and pepper. Stir in vegetables, *1½ cups* cheese and *half* of onions. Spoon into 3-quart oblong baking dish.

• Cover with foil; bake at 350°F. for 40 minutes or until vegetables are tender.

• Uncover; sprinkle remaining *½ cup* cheese and remaining onions over vegetable mixture. Bake 5 minutes more or until onions are golden. If desired, garnish with *sweet red pepper* and *fresh marjoram*.

MAKES ABOUT 8 CUPS OR 12 SERVINGS
PREP TIME: 15 MINUTES   COOK TIME: 45 MINUTES

Ginger-Cranberry Sauce

1 can (8 ounces) jellied cranberry sauce, cubed
¾ cup refrigerated MARIE'S Tangy French Dressing and Dip
1 tablespoon soy sauce
1 teaspoon ground ginger
1 teaspoon garlic powder
⅛ teaspoon ground red pepper (cayenne)

• In saucepan, mix all ingredients. Heat until cranberry sauce is melted, stirring often. Pour into bowl. Cool. Serve sauce with poultry or ham.

MAKES ABOUT 1½ CUPS
PREP TIME: 5 MINUTES   COOK TIME: 10 MINUTES   COOL TIME: 30 MINUTES

SWISS VEGETABLE BAKE

The mild, nutty taste of Swiss cheese makes this savory side dish a real crowd-pleaser. When time is short, buy Swiss cheese already shredded. An 8-ounce bag will give you the 2 cups of cheese you need to prepare this recipe.

Fiesta Potatoes

1 can (10¾ ounces) CAMPBELL'S condensed Cheddar Cheese Soup
½ cup PACE Thick & Chunky Salsa
¼ cup milk
5 medium potatoes (about 1½ pounds), cooked and sliced (about 4 cups)

• In 10-inch skillet, combine soup, salsa and milk; add potatoes, stirring gently to coat. Heat through, stirring occasionally. If desired, garnish with *cherry tomatoes* and *fresh chives.*

MAKES ABOUT 4½ CUPS OR 5 SERVINGS
PREP TIME: 25 MINUTES   COOK TIME: 10 MINUTES

No-Fuss Mac 'n' Cheese

2 cans (10¾ ounces *each*) CAMPBELL'S condensed Cream of Celery Soup
1 cup milk
1 teaspoon prepared mustard
⅛ teaspoon pepper
6 cups hot cooked elbow macaroni
  (about 3 cups dry)
4 cups shredded Cheddar cheese (1 pound)
1 can (2.8 ounces) French fried onions

• In large bowl mix soup, milk, mustard and pepper; stir in macaroni and *3 cups* cheese. Spoon into 3-quart oblong baking dish.

• Bake at 400°F. for 20 minutes or until hot and bubbling; stir. Sprinkle onions and remaining *1 cup* cheese over macaroni mixture. Bake 1 minute more or until onions are golden.

MAKES ABOUT 12 CUPS, 12 SIDE-DISH OR 8 MAIN-DISH SERVINGS
PREP TIME: 20 MINUTES   COOK TIME: 20 MINUTES

FIESTA POTATOES

The smooth flavor of Cheddar cheese and the tangy zip of salsa make this South-of-the-Border sensation a festive meal accompaniment for almost any occasion.

Isn't it romantic?
The ancient
Romans used
cinnamon to
make love
potions. More
Cinnamon
Carrots, anyone?

VEGETABLE STUFFING BAKE

1 bag (16 ounces) **PEPPERIDGE FARM** Herb Seasoned Stuffing (about 8 cups)
2 tablespoons margarine *or* butter, melted
1 can (26 ounces) **CAMPBELL'S** condensed Cream of Mushroom Soup
1 cup sour cream
3 medium zucchini, shredded (about 4 cups)
2 large carrots, shredded (about 2 cups)
1 medium onion, finely chopped (about ½ cup)

• In bowl, mix *1 cup* stuffing and margarine.

• In large bowl, mix soup and sour cream. Add zucchini, carrots, onion and remaining stuffing; toss. Spoon into 3-quart oblong baking dish. Sprinkle with reserved stuffing mixture.

• Bake at 350°F. for 35 minutes or until hot. If desired, garnish with *zucchini*, *tomato* and *fresh sage*.

MAKES ABOUT 11 CUPS OR 12 SERVINGS
PREP TIME: 15 MINUTES   COOK TIME: 35 MINUTES

CINNAMON CARROTS

1 teaspoon cornstarch
1 cup **CAMPBELL'S** Tomato Juice
3 tablespoons packed brown sugar
½ teaspoon ground cinnamon
1 package (about 16 ounces) frozen baby carrots, cooked and drained

• In saucepan, stir together cornstarch, tomato juice, brown sugar and cinnamon until smooth. Over medium heat, cook until mixture boils and thickens, stirring constantly. Add carrots. Heat through, stirring occasionally.

MAKES ABOUT 2½ CUPS OR 4 SERVINGS
PREP TIME: 5 MINUTES   COOK TIME: 15 MINUTES

Golden Broccoli Stuffing

1 bag (8 ounces) **PEPPERIDGE FARM** Corn Bread Stuffing (about 4 cups)
2 tablespoons margarine *or* butter, melted
1 can (10¾ ounces) **CAMPBELL'S** condensed Golden Corn Soup
½ cup milk
1½ cups cooked chopped broccoli
1 cup shredded Cheddar cheese (4 ounces)
½ cup diced sweet red pepper (optional)

• In small bowl, combine *1 cup* stuffing and margarine; set aside.

• In large bowl, combine soup and milk. Add broccoli, cheese, pepper and remaining stuffing; toss to mix well. Spoon into 1½-quart casserole. Sprinkle with reserved stuffing mixture.

• Bake at 350°F. for 35 minutes or until hot. If desired, garnish with *green onion* and *sweet red pepper*.

> **MAKES ABOUT 6 CUPS OR 6 SERVINGS**
> **PREP TIME: 15 MINUTES   COOK TIME: 35 MINUTES**

Broccoli Potato Topper

BROCCOLI POTATO TOPPER

1 can (19 ounces) **CAMPBELL'S CHUNKY** Chicken Broccoli Cheese Soup
1 cup cooked broccoli cuts
4 hot baked potatoes, split
Shredded Cheddar cheese

• In 1½-quart saucepan, combine soup and broccoli. Over medium heat, heat through. Serve over potatoes. Sprinkle with cheese.

> **MAKES ABOUT 3 CUPS OR 4 SERVINGS**
> **PREP TIME: 10 MINUTES   COOK TIME: 5 MINUTES**

When time to prepare supper is really short, nothing beats baking potatoes in the microwave oven. Scrub the skins, pierce with a fork and microwave 4 potatoes on HIGH power for 12-15 minutes, rearranging the potatoes once during cooking.

For the vegetables
in this recipe,
try substituting
broccoli flowerets,
cauliflowerets,
sliced celery, diced
cucumber *or* diced
zucchini.

RANCH LAYERED SALAD

8 **cups salad greens torn in bite-size pieces**
2 **cups sliced fresh mushrooms (about 6 ounces)**
2 **medium tomatoes, diced (about 2 cups)**
2 **medium carrots, shredded (about 1 cup)**
1 **cup frozen peas**
2 **green onions, chopped (about ¼ cup)**
1 **jar (12 ounces) refrigerated MARIE'S Creamy Ranch Dressing and Dip**

• In 3-quart shallow nonmetallic dish or 4-quart bowl, layer salad greens, mushrooms, tomatoes, carrots, peas and onions. Spoon dressing over salad mixture, spreading to cover top. Cover; refrigerate at least 4 hours or overnight before serving. If desired, garnish with *carrot*, *tomato* and *chicory*.

MAKES ABOUT 12 CUPS OR 12 SERVINGS
PREP TIME: 25 MINUTES   CHILL TIME: 4 HOURS

SOUPER RICE

1 **can (10½ ounces) CAMPBELL'S condensed Vegetable Soup**
1½ **soup cans water**
1 **cup uncooked regular long-grain rice**

• In 2-quart saucepan, combine soup, water and rice. Over medium heat, heat to boiling.

• Reduce heat to low. Cover; cook 20 minutes or until rice is tender and liquid is absorbed, stirring occasionally.

MAKES ABOUT 3½ CUPS OR 4 SERVINGS
PREP TIME: 5 MINUTES   COOK TIME: 25 MINUTES

APRÉS SKI
SUPPER

No-Fuss Mac
'n' Cheese
(p. 68)
•

Bean Salad
Italiano
•

Whole wheat
rolls
•

Assorted fresh
fruit

BEAN SALAD ITALIANO

¾ cup refrigerated **MARIE'S Creamy Italian Garlic Dressing and Dip**
1 can (16 ounces) **small white beans**, rinsed and drained
2 cups **cooked cut green beans**
½ cup sliced **VLASIC** *or* **EARLY CALIFORNIA pitted Ripe Olives**
1 small **red onion**, finely chopped (about ¼ cup)
⅛ teaspoon **pepper**
Salad greens

• In medium bowl, combine dressing, white beans, green beans, olives, onion and pepper; toss to coat. Cover; refrigerate at least 2 hours before serving.

• Serve on salad greens. If desired, garnish with *green onions* and *carrot curl.*

MAKES ABOUT 4 CUPS OR 8 SERVINGS
PREP TIME: 15 MINUTES   CHILL TIME: 2 HOURS

Don't care for

zucchini?

Substitute 1½ cups

cooked cut green

beans.

When selecting

fresh zucchini,

look for tender,

glossy skins free

from bruises and

blemishes. Choose

zucchini that are

slender in

diameter and

about 6 to

7 inches long.

EASY PASTA SALAD

3 **cups dry corkscrew macaroni**
1 **medium zucchini, cut in half lengthwise and thinly sliced (about 1½ cups)**
1 **cup cherry tomatoes cut in quarters**
1 **cup sliced VLASIC** *or* **EARLY CALIFORNIA pitted Ripe Olives**
½ **teaspoon dried basil leaves, crushed**
⅛ **teaspoon garlic powder**
½ **cup refrigerated MARIE'S Zesty Fat Free Red Wine Vinaigrette**

• In 4-quart saucepan, prepare macaroni according to package directions. In colander, rinse with cold water; drain well.

• In large bowl, combine macaroni, zucchini, tomatoes, olives, basil and garlic powder. Add vinaigrette; toss to coat. Cover; refrigerate at least 30 minutes before serving. If desired, garnish with *cherry tomato* and *fresh basil*.

MAKES ABOUT 7½ CUPS OR 7 SERVINGS
PREP TIME: 20 MINUTES   CHILL TIME: 30 MINUTES

HEARTY SOUPS & STEWS

Simmering soups and stews go with wintertime like hand in glove! *Chicken Chili, Mexican Beef Stew* and savory *Veal Ragout* are easy to prepare, but special enough for holidays and hearthside entertaining. Whatever the occasion, your guests will welcome the warmth and comfort of these hearty and delicious chillbusters!

Chicken Chili (page 82) and Mexican Beef Stew (page 83).

CHICKEN CHILI

1 tablespoon vegetable oil
1 pound skinless, boneless chicken breasts, cut into 1-inch pieces
1 tablespoon chili powder
1 can (10¾ ounces) CAMPBELL'S condensed Cream of Chicken Soup
1 pouch CAMPBELL'S Dry Onion with Chicken Broth Soup and Recipe Mix
2 cups water
2 cans (about 16 ounces *each*) white kidney (cannellini) beans,
　　rinsed and drained

• In 3-quart saucepan over medium heat, in hot oil, cook chicken with chili powder 5 minutes, stirring often.

• Stir in chicken soup, soup mix and water. Heat to boiling. Reduce heat to low. Cover; cook 10 minutes, stirring occasionally. Add beans. Heat through, stirring occasionally. If desired, garnish with *sour cream*, *fresh parsley* and *hot peppers*.

MAKES ABOUT 7 CUPS OR 5 MAIN-DISH SERVINGS
PREP TIME: 10 MINUTES　　COOK TIME: 25 MINUTES

MEXICAN BEEF STEW

1½ pounds ground beef
  1 large onion, chopped (about 1 cup)
 ¼ teaspoon garlic powder *or* 2 cloves garlic, minced
  1 can (10¾ ounces) CAMPBELL'S condensed Tomato Soup
  1 can (10½ ounces) CAMPBELL'S condensed Beef Broth
  1 cup water
  4 medium potatoes, cut into cubes (about 3 cups)
  2 tablespoons chili powder
  1 can (about 15 ounces) whole kernel corn, drained
     Shredded Cheddar cheese

• In 3-quart saucepan over medium-high heat, cook beef, onion and garlic powder until beef is browned and onion is tender, stirring to separate meat. Spoon off fat.

• Add soup, broth, water, potatoes and chili powder. Heat to boiling. Reduce heat to low. Cover; cook 15 minutes or until potatoes are tender, stirring occasionally.

• Add corn. Heat through, stirring occasionally. Sprinkle with cheese. If desired, garnish with *green onion*.

MAKES ABOUT 8 CUPS OR 6 MAIN-DISH SERVINGS
PREP TIME: 15 MINUTES   COOK TIME: 35 MINUTES

MEXICAN BEEF STEW

Here's a hot tip:
Chili powder
comes from the
combination of
dried chilies,
cumin, coriander,
cloves, oregano
and garlic. Use
hot chili powder
for a spicier stew.

Savory Chicken Stew

1 tablespoon vegetable oil
1 pound skinless, boneless chicken breasts, cut into 1-inch pieces
1 can (10¾ ounces) CAMPBELL'S condensed
   Cream of Chicken & Broccoli Soup
½ cup milk
4 small red potatoes, cut into quarters (about 2½ cups)
2 medium carrots, sliced (about 1 cup)
1 cup fresh broccoli flowerets
⅛ teaspoon pepper

• In 10-inch skillet over medium-high heat, in hot oil, cook *half* of the chicken until browned, stirring often. Remove; set aside. Repeat with remaining chicken. Pour off fat.

• In same skillet, combine soup, milk, potatoes, carrots, broccoli and pepper. Heat to boiling. Reduce heat to low. Cover; cook 15 minutes, stirring occasionally.

• Return chicken to skillet. Cover; cook 5 minutes or until chicken is no longer pink and vegetables are tender, stirring occasionally. If desired, sprinkle with *cracked black pepper*.

MAKES ABOUT 5½ CUPS OR 4 MAIN-DISH SERVINGS
PREP TIME: 15 MINUTES   COOK TIME: 35 MINUTES

SAVORY CHICKEN
STEW

Diehard winter sports enthusiasts sometimes just don't know when to come in from the cold. Thaw out the frosty frolickers with this rich, satisfying chillbuster of a stew and some warm, crusty French bread or breadsticks.

Bean and Pasta Soup

Bean and
Pasta Soup

2 tablespoons olive *or* vegetable oil

2 medium zucchini, cut in half lengthwise and thickly sliced (about 3 cups)

½ teaspoon dried basil leaves, crushed

¼ teaspoon garlic powder *or* 2 cloves garlic, minced

2 cans (10½ ounces *each*) CAMPBELL'S condensed Chicken Broth

1 soup can water

1 can (about 16 ounces) tomatoes, undrained and cut up

½ cup dry elbow twist *or* corkscrew macaroni

1 can (about 15 ounces) kidney beans, rinsed and drained
   Grated Parmesan cheese

• In 4-quart saucepan over medium heat, in hot oil, cook zucchini, basil and garlic powder until tender-crisp, stirring often.

• Add broth, water and *undrained* tomatoes. Heat to boiling. Add macaroni. Reduce heat to low. Cook 10 minutes or until macaroni is tender, stirring occasionally. Add beans. Heat through, stirring occasionally. Sprinkle with cheese. If desired, garnish with *fresh basil*.

MAKES ABOUT 8 CUPS OR 5 SIDE-DISH SERVINGS
PREP TIME: 10 MINUTES   COOK TIME: 25 MINUTES

Outdoors on the job, in the stands or on the sidelines, this winter-warming soup is a terrific travelling companion. Take it along in an insulated container and give yourself a reheating whenever the bluster turns into an icy blast.

❖

HEARTHSIDE
SUPPER

Veal Ragout
•
Spinach salad
•
French bread
•
Pecan pie and
ice cream

VEAL RAGOUT

  2 tablespoons olive *or* vegetable oil
1½ pounds veal for stew, cut into 1-inch pieces
  1 can (10¾ ounces) CAMPBELL'S condensed Creamy Chicken Mushroom Soup
  ½ cup water
  ½ cup Chablis *or* other dry white wine
  1 teaspoon lemon juice
  ½ teaspoon dried rosemary leaves, crushed
  ¼ teaspoon pepper
  ⅛ teaspoon garlic powder *or* 1 clove
       garlic, minced
  3 medium carrots, sliced (about 1½ cups)
  1 cup small fresh mushrooms cut in half

• In 4-quart Dutch oven over medium-high heat, in hot oil, cook *half* of the veal until browned, stirring often. Remove; set aside. Repeat with remaining veal. Pour off fat.

• In same Dutch oven, combine soup, water, wine, lemon juice, rosemary, pepper and garlic powder; add carrots. Heat to boiling. Return veal to Dutch oven. Reduce heat to low. Cover; cook 45 minutes, stirring occasionally. Uncover; add mushrooms. Cook 15 minutes or until slightly thickened and veal is fork-tender, stirring occasionally. If desired, garnish with *fresh parsley*.

MAKES ABOUT 4 CUPS OR 4 MAIN-DISH SERVINGS
PREP TIME: 15 MINUTES   COOK TIME: 1 HOUR 15 MINUTES

CREAMY POTATO SOUP

1 tablespoon margarine *or* butter
1 rib celery, sliced (about ½ cup)
4 green onions, sliced (about ½ cup)
1 can (10½ ounces) CAMPBELL'S condensed Chicken Broth
½ cup water
3 medium potatoes, peeled and sliced (about 3 cups)
⅛ teaspoon pepper
1½ cups milk

• In 2-quart saucepan over medium heat, in hot margarine, cook celery and onions until tender, stirring often. Add broth, water, potatoes and pepper. Heat to boiling. Reduce heat to low. Cover; cook 15 minutes or until potatoes are tender, stirring occasionally. Remove from heat.

• In covered blender or food processor, blend *half* of soup mixture and *¾ cup* milk until smooth. Pour into bowl. Repeat with remaining soup mixture and remaining *¾ cup* milk. Return all to saucepan. Over medium heat, heat through, stirring occasionally. If desired, garnish with *fresh chives*.

MAKES ABOUT 5 CUPS OR 5 SIDE-DISH SERVINGS
PREP TIME: 15 MINUTES   COOK TIME: 30 MINUTES

Ireland's abundant potato crop has become a popular symbol of its culture and cuisine the world over. Your St. Patrick's Day crowd will love this rich, sumptuous soup either as a meal in itself with traditional Irish soda bread, or served along with customary Celtic dishes like corned beef and cabbage.

Weights & Measures

Solid Measurements

dash = pinch

generous dash = large pinch (about $\frac{1}{16}$ teaspoon)

3 teaspoons = 1 tablespoon

4 tablespoons = $\frac{1}{4}$ cup

$5\frac{1}{3}$ tablespoons = $\frac{1}{3}$ cup

8 tablespoons = $\frac{1}{2}$ cup

$10\frac{2}{3}$ tablespoons = $\frac{2}{3}$ cup

12 tablespoons = $\frac{3}{4}$ cup

16 tablespoons = 1 cup

1 ounce = 28.35 grams

1 pound = 453.59 grams

1 gram = 0.035 ounce

1 kilogram = 2.2 pounds

Liquid Measurements

1 tablespoon = $\frac{1}{2}$ fluid ounce

2 tablespoons = 1 fluid ounce

1 cup = 8 fluid ounces

1 cup = $\frac{1}{2}$ pint

2 cups = 1 pint = 16 fluid ounces

2 pints = 1 quart = 32 fluid ounces

4 quarts = 1 gallon = 128 fluid ounces

8 quarts = 1 peck

2 gallons = 1 peck

4 pecks = 1 bushel

Useful Equivalents

$\frac{1}{8}$ teaspoon = 0.5 milliliter (mL)

$\frac{1}{4}$ teaspoon = 1 milliliter (mL)

$\frac{1}{2}$ teaspoon = 2 milliliters (mL)

1 teaspoon = 5 milliliters (mL)

1 tablespoon = 15 milliliters (mL)

$\frac{1}{4}$ cup = 2 fluid ounces = 50 milliliters (mL)

$\frac{1}{3}$ cup = 3 fluid ounces = 75 milliliters (mL)

$\frac{1}{2}$ cup = 4 fluid ounces = 125 milliliters (mL)

1 cup = 8 fluid ounces = 250 milliliters (mL)

1 quart = 946.4 milliliters (mL)

1 liter = 1.06 quart

STORING PERISHABLE FOODS

Follow these guidelines for storing perishable foods in the refrigerator or in the freezer.
- Raw meat and poultry should be wrapped securely so juices do not leak and contaminate other foods or surfaces. Since repeated handling can introduce bacteria to meat and poultry, it's best to leave the product in the store wrap unless the wrap is torn. Use plastic bags over commercial packaging.
- Date purchased food items and be sure to use them within the recommended time.
- Eggs should be stored in their carton in the refrigerator, not in the door.
- Arrange items in the refrigerator or freezer to allow air to circulate evenly.

FOOD STORAGE CHART*

These short but safe storage time limits will help keep refrigerated food from spoiling. The time limits given for frozen foods are to maintain maximum peak flavor and texture.

Product	Refrigerator (40°F.)	Freezer (0°F.)
Eggs		
Fresh, in shell	3 weeks	Don't freeze
Raw yolks, whites	2-4 days	1 year
Hard-cooked	1 week	Don't freeze well
Soups & Stews		
Vegetable or meat-added	3-4 days	2-3 months
Meats & Poultry		
Bacon	7 days	1 month
Beef roasts	3-5 days	6-12 months
Beef steaks	3-5 days	6-12 months
Chicken or turkey pieces	1-2 days	9 months
Chicken or turkey, whole	1-2 days	1 year
Ground beef, lamb, pork, poultry or mixtures of them	1-2 days	3-4 months
Ham, canned, label says "keep refrigerated"	6-9 months	Don't freeze
Ham, fully cooked, slices	3-4 days	1-2 months
Lamb chops	3-5 days	6-9 months
Pork chops	3-5 days	4-6 months
Pork roasts	3-5 days	4-6 months
Sausage, raw—beef, pork or poultry	1-2 days	1-2 months
Smoked breakfast links or patties	7 days	1-2 months
Stew meat—beef, lamb or pork	1-2 days	3-4 months
Cooked Meats & Poultry		
Gravy or meat broth	1-2 days	2-3 months
Meat or meat mixtures	3-4 days	2-3 months
Poultry mixtures	3-4 days	4-6 months
Poultry pieces covered with broth/gravy	1-2 days	6 months
Poultry pieces, plain	3-4 days	4 months

*Source: U.S. Department of Agriculture-Food Safety and Inspection Service.

RECIPES BY PRODUCT INDEX

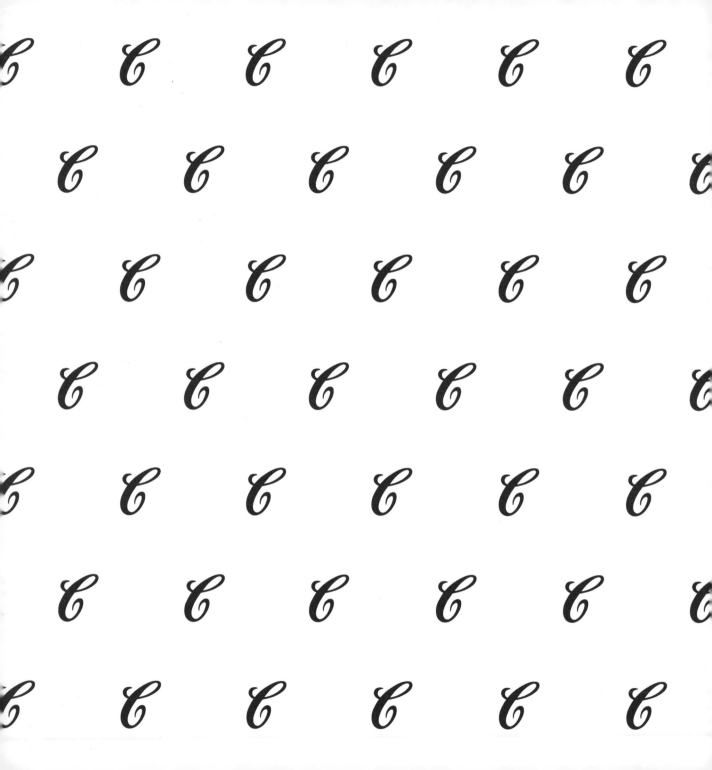